GET
OUT!

GET OUT!

150 Easy Ways for Kids and Grown-Ups to Get Into Nature and Build a Greener Future

Judy Molland

free spirit
PUBLISHING®

Library of Congress Cataloging-in-Publication Data
  Molland, Judy.
    Get out! : 150 ways for kids & grown-ups to get into nature and build a greener future / Judy Molland.
       p. cm.
    ISBN 978-1-57542-335-7
     1. Green movement—Popular works. 2. Sustainable living—Popular works. 3. Environmental protection—Citizen participation. I. Title.
    GE195.M65 2009
    333.72—dc22   2009017352

Edited by Eric Braun
Cover and interior design by Tasha Kenyon
Photos on pages 18, 22, 31, 38, 50, 63, 87, and 97 © istockphoto.com
Photos on pages 34, 53, 66, 94, and 100 © dreamstime.com
Photo on page 26 © D'Lee Dreyer
All other photos © Tasha Kenyon

Statistics cited on pages 1–2 are from the Kaiser Family Foundation, the University of Maryland, Playing for Keeps, and Andrew Balmford, et al.

10 9 8 7 6 5 4 3 2 1
Printed in the United States of America

Free Spirit Publishing Inc.
217 Fifth Avenue North, Suite 200
Minneapolis, MN 55401-1299
(612) 338-2068
help4kids@freespirit.com
www.freespirit.com

As a member of the Green Press Initiative, Free Spirit Publishing is committed to the three Rs: Reduce, Reuse, Recycle. Whenever possible, we print our books on recycled paper containing a minimum of 30% post-consumer waste. At Free Spirit it's our goal to nurture not only children, but nature too!

green press INITIATIVE

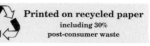

Printed on recycled paper
including 30%
post-consumer waste

Dedication

To Joe, who introduced me to the magnificent Sierra Nevada Mountains and changed my life forever.

Acknowledgments

I am grateful to Judy Galbraith and John Kober of Free Spirit for giving me the opportunity to write about a topic that impassions me. A huge thank you to my husband Joe and my son Will for living this book with me and providing the necessary emotional, technical, and intellectual support, not to mention some great hikes and some excellent dinners.

The genesis for this book came from an article on science education that I wrote for Dominion Parenting Media, and I am grateful to my editors there, Bill Lindsay and Deirdre Wilson, for starting me out on this path. In the course of writing that article and researching for this book, I have been motivated by several experts: Richard Louv, Janice Koch, and Judi Opert Sandler have been especially inspirational.

Thanks also go to the many friends and colleagues who have supported me in this project: in particular Bernadette Suski Harding, Martha Jackson, Ellen Nordberg, Laurie Scheer, Janet Simms, Matthew Simms, and Caroline Smith. And where would I be without my amazing editor, Eric Braun, whose excellence and insights have been integral to the final shape of this book? Thank you, Eric!

Lastly, a note of love and gratitude to my mother, whose love for our native Devon, England, has stayed with me all these years.

Contents

Introduction

Do you remember playing outside? Maybe you remember leaving home on a summer morning and not returning except for meals until bedtime. You might have fond memories of a favorite outdoor place where you and your friends played and explored. Maybe it was a park, maybe it was a beach or wooded area. Maybe it was nothing but a field of weeds, but it was yours, it was outdoors, and you loved it.

Kids now are much less likely to have such a personal connection with nature. And how could they? Their outdoor time is, generally speaking, sporadic and highly supervised. Recent studies have revealed that:

- Children between the ages of 8 and 18 spend an average of 6.5 hours a day staring at electronic screens (television, video games, computers, etc.), leaving little time for outdoor play.

- The number of children who participated in outdoor activities such as hiking, walking, and fishing dropped by 50 percent between 1997 and 2003.

- 80 percent of children under age 2 and more than 60 percent of children ages 2 to 5 lack daily access to outdoor play.

- Children between the ages of 8 and 11 can identify significantly more artificial Pokemon characters than real, native living things, such as oak trees, sparrows, and otters.

In schools, hours devoted to physical education and recess are down compared to previous generations; and at home, parents are more reluctant than ever to let kids spend time outside unsupervised.

Yet many reasons exist why a connection to nature is crucial for children:

- Physical development: Being connected to nature may keep kids in better shape and help in the fight against obesity. Watch a group of children in a wooded area as they run, jump, and climb over things. They are exercising!

- Cognitive development: Studies show that just being exposed to nature can improve memory, concentration, and grades. The pace of play in nature is self-regulated and thus can increase attention span and stimulate the senses.

- Social development: Nature reduces stress, soothes the psyche, and eases tensions, paving the way for improved communication and closer bonding with others.

- Green development: Children are responsible for the future of our planet. An early connection to nature leads children to grow up as better stewards of the environment.

- Spiritual development: Nature stirs youngsters to question their place in the world and to wonder at the magnificence of their surroundings. A child's imagination is turned on, an important part of overall development.

The simple fact is that nature is awesome. It's amazing to look at, touch, and listen to. It's wondrous and remarkably self-sufficient.

One thing has improved with time: Modern kids are more likely than previous generations to understand concerns about the environment and their roles in preserving it. Of course that's important. But if a child can describe how global warming is affecting our planet but can't remember the last time he explored woods or a beach, he's not likely to genuinely care about nature. According to research conducted at Cornell University, children who spend time in nature before age 11 are much more likely to grow up to be environmentally minded adults than kids who don't.

On a personal note, I gain so much pleasure from being outdoors that I want others to have that experience too. As a mother, I have seen nature's positive, calming effect on my children and their friends, and it worries me that we are getting further away from nature. I know I always feel better when I have spent time outdoors, stepping on the earth. As the poet Terry Tempest Williams wrote, "Nature quiets the mind by engaging with an intelligence larger than our own." Getting out makes common sense, in more ways than one.

Get Out!

With all this in mind, I searched for a single resource that would provide lots of simple, practical tips to help me get my own children and my students more in touch with nature and help us all become more eco-friendly.

I couldn't find one. That's why I wrote this book. On every page, you'll find straightforward, engaging activities, projects, games, ideas, and tips to help you get yourself and your kids outdoors, improve your physical and spiritual health, and do more for Earth—150 doable ideas, all in one place. Whether you live in the heart of a big city, an outlying suburb, a small village, or a rural area, there is something here for you.

Get Out! is intended for use by parents, grandparents, teachers, counselors, youth leaders, and any other adults who spend time with kids. Maybe you're a stay-at-home dad looking for a few ways to get your toddler outside during the week. Or you're a teacher or youth group leader, and you have a bunch of kids with a whole lot of energy. Or you're a grandparent who wants to share your love of the outdoors with your grandkids. Maybe you're a homeschooler looking to inject some eco-knowledge into your curriculum. Whether you're looking at one child or a big group, most of the ideas in *Get Out!* will work for you. If you read ahead of time and make adjustments for the size and age of your group, the ideas can be used with one kid or 30. When you see the words "your kids," think of the group, small or large, with whom you're sharing these activities.

You don't have to revamp your lifestyle if you want to connect more with nature and do more for the environment. This book is about finding new, simple, fulfilling ways to do a little extra, to take the next step—wherever it is you currently stand. Take a step now, take another later, and when your kids grow up, *getting out* will be built into their sensibilities.

Get the Best Results

As you prepare to get out with your kids, be careful not to push for too much at once. Especially if a child is reluctant, it's best to choose one or two ideas to start with. Here are some tips to help you succeed:

- **Show enthusiasm.** Try to make it fun, and remember a sense of humor! Kids won't embrace a project if it seems like homework or medicine.

- **Be curious.** You don't have to know everything about nature in order to engage your kids: learn together. Learn through experience.

- **Share your precious nature-based memories.** Most kids love to hear about what grown-ups were like when *they* were kids, so tell about a tree you loved to climb, a stream you always waded in, or vacations you took.

- **Be ready to compromise.** Tell your child that you love the computer (for example) as much as she does, and you can have time for technology and the great outdoors. Make a schedule together for screen time and outdoor time, and do your best to stick to it.

- **Finally, be flexible.** If things aren't going the way you planned, adjust. Figure out what *is* working— or what might. Don't have preconceived ideas of what success looks like.

Even with all the ideas here, this book only scratches the surface—like a garden trowel scraping a handful of soil from the earth. You can find a whole planet full of other ways to get out, if only you dig. I'm sure you can come up with lots more! I'd love to hear about them. You can write to me at:

Free Spirit Publishing
217 Fifth Avenue North, Suite 200
Minneapolis, MN 55401-1299
help4kids@freespirit.com

Get Started
Cool Ways to Embrace Nature *Today*

Get started now! Nature is close at hand—at the park or playground, on your balcony, in your window box, in the yard, on the boulevard, even growing in the sidewalk cracks. Whether kids are collecting fallen leaves, catching snowflakes for the first time, or playing in the waves at the beach, there is beauty and wonder in watching them discover the world around them.

One thing kids don't need is too much guidance. Encourage even the youngest children to explore whatever attracts them, then stand back and let them do it. This chapter provides 35 things you and your kids can do today—right now—to get out and enjoy nature.

1 *Lead by example.* Want your kids to value nature? Want them to discover for themselves how amazing the natural world can be, and how much fun it is to play in the dirt, roll down a grassy bank, and find slimy slugs after the rain? Nothing sends a stronger message than if they see you out there enjoying yourself, so step outside. Build a sandcastle! Make a snowperson! Rub your toes in the grass. Remember: Enthusiasm is contagious.

---

*When you see the words
"your kids," think of the group, small or large,
with whom you're sharing these activities.*

---

2 *Follow by example, too.* Most grown-ups can learn something from kids. They are receptive to new things. They're curious. Be receptive and curious, too! Ask questions. Encourage questions. If you don't know the answer, admit it. Look it up together. Or make up a story. *This seaweed is a monster's hair. These rocks are from the walls of an ancient castle.* Here's a fun game: Find a creek, pond, park, or any place with lots of life, appoint a leader among the kids, and follow him. If he stops to turn over a log to see what's beneath it, everyone else looks, too. If he throws stones in the lake, so do the rest of you. If he digs in the mud and gets his pants dirty—don't hold back.

3 *Turn a walk into a safari.* You can do this with babies, teenagers, and anyone else who likes a good stroll. Head to a park or path, or simply take the sidewalk by your home. Even in big cities you'll see birds, bugs, shrubs, and trees—take a closer look when you pass. Better yet: stop and examine them. Bring a magnifying glass to really zoom in. You can also chat with kids about things you never seem to talk about during the busy days—or just be quiet and listen to the squirrels chirp and the leaves rattle in the trees.

4 *Let kids set the pace.* If your four-year-old resists the idea of a long walk, keep it short and make it fun. Play "I Spy" or another game. Take a healthy snack and stop in the grass to enjoy it together—especially if your child gets tired. And if it's hard tearing older children away from video games or texting, go easy. Let them know that time in nature is like health food for the brain, and you'd like to make a schedule everyone agrees to so time indoors is balanced with time outside.

5 *Be prepared.* When you're outdoors with kids, make sure you have what you need to make it a safe, enjoyable, and generally positive outing. Carry water and a first aid kit, and make sure everyone wears sunblock to protect them from UV rays. Bug spray will keep the irritating bug bites to a minimum, and if you're on the water, everyone needs a life jacket. If needed, collect permission slips and waivers.

6 *Collect stones.* Children love gathering rocks. A great place to find rocks is a quarry, but get permission from the land owner first. Rivers and wave-swept beaches—where rocks are pushed around and smoothed over the years—are also good. Smooth or jagged, striped or plain, colorful or gray . . . how many types can you find? What's your favorite? And why limit yourself to stones? You can also collect shells, fossils, feathers, pinecones, or leaves, depending on where you live and the time of year.

7 *Respect nature.* When collecting stones or other things, be thoughtful about what you pick up. Think: what are the consequences of taking this? Never pick flowers or leaves from living plants (unless you have permission), and make sure you know what's allowed where you are. Many places have a "Take nothing but photos, leave nothing but footprints" rule. You can always choose to take pictures of stones or just take one really cool one.

8 *Become part of your surroundings.* You can do this in a forest, at a beach, in a park, along a riverbank, or anywhere else you can find flora and fauna. Walk quietly into the area and choose a comfortable place to sit. Then, be as still as possible. Don't even turn your head. Imagine you are part of the natural environment, and soak in the sights, sounds, and smells around you. If the local animals scattered when you came, they'll soon get back to their daily business. They may even approach you.

9 *Play Camouflage Tag.* All you need is a few people and an area with good hiding places, such as a playground, park, or wooded area. The person who is "it"—the seeker—closes her eyes and counts to 50 while everyone else hides. The catch is that each player must be able to see her from his hiding spot. When the seeker opens her eyes, she yells, "Camouflage!" and holds up one to five fingers. Staying where she is, she looks around and shouts out the name of whomever she sees. The last person she spots wins—but only if he can say from where he is how many fingers she has up. He's next!

10

Listen to the birds. See if you can figure out when birds are most and least vocal or how their songs vary by time of day. Can you isolate the sounds of one particular bird and identify which one it is? Of course, you might also hear nonvocal communications such as a woodpecker's bill hammering or a hummingbird's whirring wings.

11 *Identify bird songs and bird calls.* Most birds make two types of sounds: songs and calls. Songs are more musical and complex, and are generally created by male birds attracting mates or defending territory. Bird calls are simpler, and are used by both sexes to communicate information. There are calls for aggression, warning, identification, to announce location or a food source, and many other purposes.

12 *Listen to singing frogs.* Take a flashlight to the pond on a night in spring or early summer, and you may hear frogs singing. These are male frogs trying to attract mates, and they may pipe down when they hear you coming. Don't worry, though. Just be still and wait. Moments later, they'll start up again—they don't want any females to miss them! Sweep your flashlight beam over the shallow edge of the water to find the frogs.

13 *Find squirrel highways.* Most squirrels stay in a relatively small area, usually about an acre, their whole lives. They know that area very well, including every branch of the trees they roam. If they didn't have the branches memorized, they couldn't skitter along them at the high speeds they sometimes do—when escaping a predator, for instance, or when a dominant male wants to

intimidate a younger male. Watch the squirrels in your yard or at a park for a while and see if you can identify the squirrels' favorite routes—or "squirrel highways."

14 *Keep a nature journal.* Make nature journals using recycled paper. Revisit the same place in your backyard, school grounds, or park throughout the year—perhaps once a week—and note the changes you observe in the weather, trees, animal activity, and anything else you notice. You can write paragraphs or poems, make lists, or sketch pictures. Every few months, go back to your notes and drawings to see how things have changed. Nature writing and sketching can help you and your kids slow down, focus, and increase your awareness of the natural world. What a great antidote to the daily hurry-hurry-hurry mode.

15 ***Get to know local trees.*** Wherever you live, there are probably trees in your area. Take a close look at a few. Are they all the same? What's different about them? Compare the leaves—are they jagged-edged or smooth-edged? Are they each in one piece or do they have leaflets? How about the bark, buds, or flowers (depending on the time of year)? Collect the different leaves you find on the ground, but be sure not to pull them off the branches, which can hurt the trees. Borrow a nature guide from the library to identify species, or check with your local Department of Parks and Recreation to find guided nature walks where foliage is identified.

16 *Attract birds.* Design and plant a garden or window box full of brightly colored flowers—even two or three pots on the window ledge can do the trick—and wait for the birds to come. Most wild birds are attracted to brightly colored gardens, and planting annuals is an easy way to make one. Sunflowers, zinnias, and asters are all sun-loving annuals. You can select flowers and plants that appeal to a range of birds, or plan to attract certain species, like finches or hummingbirds, with specific flowers. Check out www.enature.com to get more information about what flowers attract what birds. Consult a gardening zone guide (available at a local nursery) to choose varieties that grow well in your area. Be sure to plant your garden or window box where you can observe it regularly and enjoy all your new visitors. When it comes to feeding birds, nothing beats native vegetation. If you plant a variety of native plants, they can provide birds with food at different times of the year in the form of fruit and seeds. Native plants are also home to tasty invertebrates like bugs and spiders. Your visitors will love those!

17 *Attract butterflies.* Butterflies love colorful flowers, too, especially zinnias. You can also plant butterfly bushes, which remain evergreen year-round in mild climates. Get a good pair of binoculars and admire the beauty of butterflies close up.

18 *Adopt a piece of the earth.* Walk around your yard, neighborhood, or school and find an area that needs attention. (If you're not sure whether it's public or private property, check with your local city council to clarify.) It might be a place that is littered with trash or has no plants on it. Here are some things your kids can do:

- Pick up litter and put up "Please don't litter" signs.
- Plant grass or flower seeds to help save the soil.
- Plant shrubs or trees to provide food and shelter for birds.
- Hang a bird feeder from a pole or tree to give birds food all year round; keep the feeder clean to help birds stay healthy.

19 *Go to a nature center.* These often have open areas where kids can play and explore, while adults can sit and watch without hovering. Or follow a guided trail and find out about the plants and animals that call the nature center home. Botanical gardens are also a great place to learn about your local flora.

20 *Explore a wildlife rescue center.* These centers treat sick and injured wild animals, and they raise orphaned birds and mammals until they are old enough to survive on their own. If you want to do more than visit, most rescue centers have volunteer opportunities for people ages 13 and up (teens may need to be supervised by a parent or leader). As volunteers, you could be involved in animal care, wildlife calls, gardening, or feeding the animals.

21 *Have a picnic.* Pack your meal—perhaps salads and sandwiches—in reusable containers, take along a cloth tablecloth and napkins, and head for a local park. Make sure to bring reusable cups and plates, and recycle any plastic and glass bottles. Don't forget the deet-free bug spray to keep the critters from ruining your good time. Kick back, play soccer or tag, and enjoy nature!

22 *Have a daily "green hour."* The National Wildlife Federation recommends that parents give their kids a daily green hour—time set aside every day to play outside and interact with the natural world. This time should be unstructured (no rules) and *fun!* If you're busy, start with 15 minutes a day, and do it *every* day. If kids are reluctant, show them how fun it is by joining them. Even on a wet day, you can still get out and play together as long as you're dressed for the weather. As e.e. cummings wrote, the world is "mud-luscious" and "puddle-wonderful." See www.greenhour .org for more tips.

As e.e. cummings wrote, the world is "mud-luscious" and "puddle-wonderful."

---

23 *Create your own treasure hunt.* Make a list of items likely to be found in the nature of your neighborhood or play area. Next, make copies of the list for each kid or team in your group, hand out paper bags to collect the loot, and send them on their way. Kids will be more engaged if you include several weird or gross items on your list. Here are a few list-starter ideas: a dead bug, a bird feather, a leaf bigger than your hand, a worm, moss or lichen, a seed or pit, a stick shaped like the letter "y," a smooth rock, a cup of mud (bring your own cup). Depending on the age of your kids, you may want to put hunters in pairs and set firm boundaries where you can keep track of them. Remind your hunters to respect natural surroundings. You could even put "five pieces of trash" on the list.

24 *Go digital.* Instead of collecting items for a treasure hunt, have your hunters take pictures of their findings. Make it challenging! Here are some suggestions: a hole or nest in a tree, fungus on a rock, squirrels chasing each other, an animal hole in the ground, a spider web with a spider (and its prey?) inside, a tree that's shorter than the hunter, deer tracks. With your digital game, you'll also be saving paper.

25 *Camp out.* Check out nature sounds at night. If you have a backyard, pitch a tent there; if there's a patio, sleep there. This can be extra fun to do with friends or neighbors—including the adults. Now . . . what do you hear? Owls? Crickets? Frogs? Small animals searching for food? The howl of a coyote? Be sure to talk about the sounds you are hearing.

26 *Take up stargazing.* The sky at night can be spectacular, awe-inspiring, and humbling. There's nothing like lying on your back and studying the stars. Winter is a great time to do this because cold, dry air is stiller than warm air, which improves visibility and makes it easier to distinguish stars. Visit NASA's Web site (www.spaceplace.nasa.gov) and print out a constellation guide—then see how many constellations you can identify. You may even spot one of the five planets that are occasionally visible to the naked eye in our solar system: Mars, Venus, Jupiter, Saturn, and Mercury. If you live in a big city, light pollution will interfere with your sky viewing, but try observing with a blanket draped over your head to block out street lights, or head to the outskirts of your city.

27 *Try cloud watching.* If the stars by night are tricky to make out, look for shapes in the clouds instead. On a cloudy day, find a comfortable spot, spread out a blanket or towel, lie down with your kids, and see what you can see. (Make sure the sun is not shining directly in anyone's eyes.) Ask your children what shapes they can see, and encourage them to share. If you see a strange monster, a laughing face, a spaceship, a frog, or maybe an angel, tell your kids about it. Imagine that you are all traveling on a cloud. What can you see? Where are you going?

28 *Create a water patrol.* Give your children responsibility for watering plants, yards, gardens, patio planters, or window boxes. This gets them outside on a regular schedule, and they'll feel good helping out. Teach them a few tips: It's best to water plants thoroughly but less frequently to encourage deep root growth and healthier plants; it's also best to water in the early morning to prevent evaporation; and don't water on windy days when fences or sidewalks may get wetter than the ground.

29 *Get familiar with local water.* At a stream or creek, look for evidence of animals: if there are beavers, for example, you'll see dams, as well as chewed logs and branches. Can you see fish, bugs, turtles, or tadpoles in the water? By rivers and oceans, see how many different types of animals you can count along the shore, and look for tracks, shells, and crustaceans. Schools in most states and provinces have river projects in which students learn how to monitor the health of the water. They test for water level, clarity, and fecal bacteria content at least twice a year, and they learn how to restore the health of the river and become its steward. To learn of river projects in your area, contact your city, state, or province through their Web site or do an Internet search for "river project" and the name of the river you're interested in.

30 *Get wet.* Canoeing, kayaking, sailing, and swimming are great for kids of any age. As they get older, they may be up for snorkeling, scuba diving, or river rafting. These are all great ways to have fun in nature. Find excellent teachers, make sure everyone in your group knows how to swim, and of course check on the safety gear.

31 CHECK OUT WHAT'S HAPPENING AROUND THE WORLD.

→ Angie Meadows is a kindergarten teacher in Wilmington, Delaware, who teaches her students about local ecosystems and horseshoe crabs, an endangered species that has lived in the Delaware Bay for the past 300 million years. "The kindergartners have made several trips to the bay," enthuses Meadows, "and they always come back all sandy and gritty and with big smiles on their faces!" She suggests parents provide a change of clothes.

32 *Have a snow day.* Build igloos or snow caves, or go sledding or snow tubing. Or try snowshoeing—no lift tickets are required. Older kids may prefer snowboarding or downhill skiing. If they choose back-country or cross-country skiing, they will get a chance to admire the beauty of nature away from the crowds. Snow truly is a wondrous natural phenomenon and one that few kids can resist.

33 *Ride a bike.* Simply put, riding a bike is fun. Fast or slow, long trips or short, biking is pure youthful joy—and that goes for grown-ups, too. Do it whenever you can. You don't need fancy bikes, just two wheels and the open road. Learn bike safety, and always wear a helmet. *Bonus:* biking saves gas dollars as well as the environment.

34

CHECK OUT WHAT'S HAPPENING AROUND THE WORLD.

→ In many countries, more people ride bikes than drive cars. In Japan, for example, there are special parking garages for bicycles, so people can ride them to work. An estimated 3 million bikes are parked daily at rail stations, several times greater than the number of commuter cars. Other countries featuring bike parking garages include the Netherlands, Denmark, and Germany.

35

Read about nature. Maybe it's way too cold outside. Maybe it's bedtime. Hey, nobody can get out *all* the time. When you have the chance, read with your kids about nature—it's a wonderful way to spark their imaginations and spend time together. No matter the age of your kids, you can find hundreds of great books— fiction, nonfiction, or poetry—about getting out. Ask your librarian for recommendations or do an Internet search for terms you're interested in (such as "nature," "outdoor adventure," or "global warming"). And here's a fun idea: Do your reading outside.

Go Further
Projects, Plans, and Outings

If you're ready to really dig in, the ideas in this chapter will require a bit more planning and commitment, but the payoff is worth it: a deeper, healthier relationship with nature. So gather your kids and get ready to grab hold of their imaginations. This chapter provides 26 ways to see close-up the many ways nature is awesome.

36 *Raise butterflies.* Set up an aquarium or a wide-mouthed jar with netting affixed firmly on top. (Don't just punch holes in the jar lid, because it holds in too much moisture.) In early summer, hunt for caterpillars on the leaves of plants such as milkweed. Break off the leaf or gently coax the caterpillar onto a stick and put it in your jar. Provide your caterpillars with a consistent supply of fresh milkweed leaves to eat, and watch the magical changes in the butterfly's life cycle. It will take a little less than a month to go from caterpillar to chrysalis and finally to an amazing butterfly. Be sure to let the butterfly go free outside a few hours after it emerges. For more information, visit the Leave No Child Inside Web site at www.kidsoutside.info/activities/btrfly.htm. You can also purchase butterfly kits online that come complete with caterpillars. Do an Internet search for "butterfly kits."

37 *Adopt a tree.* As a group or family, choose a favorite tree you can visit often, and have children take notes by recording the diameter of the tree's trunk, the reach of its branches, and anything else they'd like to jot down. They can also make bark rubbings using crayons and paper, smell the flowers, and gather the seeds. Take a photo of your tree every week or every month, and put the pictures in a series to see how it changes over the course of a year—or longer. If something interesting happens, like a big snow or a wind storm, go to your tree and see how it was affected. Take more pictures!

38 *Plant a tree.* It's good for the environment, because trees absorb carbon dioxide, and it's an excellent way to create a lasting family memory. You will feel great about beautifying a neighborhood and providing shade as well as a home for birds and animals. Make sure to water it. Caring for a plant is a perfect way for children to learn about caring for the earth. Start by going to a nursery or gardening center and talking to the people there about what kind of tree to plant and how to nurture it.

39 *Build a bird house.* Make it a green bird house by using recycled materials. All you need is some scrap wood, nails, a hammer, and a drill. (Reserve the hammering and drilling for older kids or adults.) An Internet search for "build a bird house" will provide dozens of options for building plans. Once you've finished, place the house in a safe location and wait for the nesting to start.

40 ***Feed the birds.*** Make your own bird feeders and hang them near windows for indoor bird watching. You can make one out of a paper milk carton by cutting openings on opposite sides, where birds will reach in for the seed. For a perch, poke holes under the openings and insert a piece of dowel all the way through. Finally, coat the carton with nontoxic, weatherproof paint and glue craft stick shingles onto the roof. Fill the bottom of your feeder with birdseed mix (black sunflower seeds work best). Another option is to roll a pinecone in peanut butter and coat it with birdseed, attach it to a string, and hang it outside. Sit by your window and enjoy the action!

41 *Plant natural bird and butterfly feeders.* Many shrubs and trees produce berries for birds to eat—go to a garden store to find out what works in your climate. These not only feed birds, but also provide them with shelter . . . and make your yard look great. While you're at the store, ask about planting butterfly bushes, another great way to attract life to your growing area. Hummingbirds and beneficial insects, as well as butterflies, are attracted by the nectar-rich flowers of these bushes.

42 *Create an owl box.* Owls do not build their own nests—most simply use the old nests of other birds. But some, such as barn owls and screech owls, are called *cavity nesters* because they will nest in open artificial cavities. If you live in the right area, you can attract these beautiful birds by building or buying an owl box. (Barn owls live in meadows and fields all over North America, and screech owls, which are bigger and prey on barn owls, live in wooded areas in North and South America.) Responsibilities come with an owl box, such as cleaning it out once a year. Make sure you talk to your neighbors, too. Barn owls can be quite noisy at night during breeding and nesting seasons. Visit the Hungry Owl Project at www.hungryowl.org for more information.

43 *Build a bat house.* Did you know that a single brown bat can eat up to 1,000 mosquitoes in an hour? You can attract bats to your neighborhood by building a bat house, which will provide you with natural pest control and provide bats—many species of which are endangered—with a safe home. Bat houses can be many sizes, from about 2' x 3' and up. Place yours in the sun and at least 12 feet off the ground to prevent predators from gaining entrance. For free bat house plans, check out http://free.woodworking-plans.org/bat-house-plans.html.

44 *Dig, plant, grow.* A vegetable garden can be great fun as well as educational. Kids gain firsthand experience of life cycles and learn patience and responsibility as they see how their care affects the garden. Of course you also get fresh, delicious food (kids who resist store-bought veggies may find their own product much tastier). Let younger kids get dirty by pushing seeds into holes, while older kids can help map, dig, plant, water, weed, and harvest. Avoid synthetic pesticides, herbicides, or inorganic fertilizers that can pollute soil and water. Learn everything you need to know about planting and tending vegetables at www.backyardgardener.com/veg or www.thegardenhelper.com/vegetables.html.

45 *Put it in the window.* Have no yard? Not even a patio? Don't worry: You and your kids can work the earth of your own salad garden even if you live in an apartment the size of a salad bowl. All you need is one sunny window and window box planters or pots at least 8 inches deep with holes for drainage. Add potting soil enriched with compost and seeds. Radishes, mesclun mix, and baby carrots would all make a good start. Follow the directions on the seed packets, and you should be able to harvest your delicious salad within about a month. (For bigger carrots, let them grow longer.) Keep track of growth with your kids.

46 *Turn your schoolyard or community into a classroom.* A school or community garden has many benefits. It's a great way for kids to learn about food from seed to table, and it also encourages healthier eating—for kids *and* adults. And it strengthens community by bringing people together for fun and for a common goal. Your kids can explore, touch, smell, and taste the food you grow, and your garden will beautify the area, too. Start by finding educators or community members who will support the garden, and develop a proposal. You'll want to research the best location and what grows well in your area. If it's a school project, you'll need to plan for maintenance over summer break.

47 *Put nature on the calendar.* Together with another family—or two or three or more—arrange a regular "Outdoors Date." Depending on the weather and the ages and interests of your participants, this could be as simple as meeting at the playground every week or month, or something heartier, like a series of hikes or an ongoing flag football game. Do the same thing every meeting or let a different participant choose each meeting's activity. The important thing is that once it's on the calendar, and others are depending on you,

you're less likely to skip it. Invite grandparents, cousins, and other family members to join in.

48 **Bring out the strollers.** If your little ones are too small for more active Outdoors Dates, organize a stroller group instead. Meet for weekly nature walks, even if "nature" means checking out the park or strolling down the block. Start with short hikes and go for enjoyment, not endurance. Be prepared—the right shoes, enough water, and some healthy snacks all go a long way toward ensuring a positive experience for everyone. Stop to let the kids dig up some bugs or lift a log or two before heading home. Make sure it's fun for everyone: remember, you're modeling a love of the outdoors. Keep it on the calendar and don't skip!

49 **Become nature detectives.** Track animals in your own neighborhood by finding tracks of dogs, cats, squirrels, rabbits, and birds. It's easiest to spot them in snow, dirt, mud, and the edges of puddles, ponds, and lakes. Get on your knees and look closely for animal signs: besides tracks, look for feathers, scat, broken twigs, and bent grass where animals have trod or lain down. Kids of all ages can track. Some camps and wilderness-training schools teach sophisticated tracking techniques to older children. Be sure not to reach inside any animal's den, if your tracking leads you there. If your kids are keeping journals (see page 15), record dates and types of tracks, and include any photos you've taken along the way.

50 Do deeper investigation. Continuing the detective work, find out even more about your local flora and fauna by checking out a field guide from a library or nature center. Take it with you on your next excursion, and use it to identify the grasses, flowers, trees, animals, birds, and bugs you spot. When kids study nature closely—and understand what they're looking at—they're on the path to becoming stewards of the planet. To get an online look at your area, go to www.enature .com. Typing in your zip code will give you an exhaustive look at all the animals and plants in your locality (United States only). Very cool!

Take a field guide with you on your next excursion, and use it to identify the grasses, flowers, trees, animals, birds, and bugs you spot.

51 *Join a mycological group.* Love mush-rooms? Learn everything you ever wanted to know about mushrooms, especially those in your area, by joining a mycological club. Mycology is the study of fungi. Do an Internet search for groups near you, and you can join like-minded mushroom-lovers in hunting, growing, eating, and photographing mushrooms. Be careful, though: never pick mushrooms if you're not sure what kind they are. It's best to go mushroom hunting with someone experienced.

52 *Take nature and wildlife photog-raphy.* Now that you're becoming experts on your local environment, you will want to take some pictures! Everyone from small children to adults can do this, and it will develop the habit of looking closely at the world. Digital cameras are portable and increasingly affordable. For first-time users, review a few basics: remember that light must be on your subject, not coming from behind it; decide what you want to focus on in your picture; consider whether the camera should be horizontal or vertical. After that, let your crew go and take photos of ducks on a lake, ladybugs on a leaf, sunsets, sunrises, weirdly shaped trees, or whatever intrigues them. As a final step, they can proudly post their images on a classroom or family Web site.

53 *Go camping.* It's a great way to utterly immerse yourselves in nature, get out of your routines, talk to each other, relax, and set kids on the path to a lifetime of adventure. If you can't get away for long, or if you're a nervous novice, even one night away feels great. You can rent basic gear such as a tent, sleeping bags, and a stove at many outdoors stores. Be sure to bring extra clothing (including warm clothing and rain gear), flashlights, insect repellent, sunscreen, a first aid kit, toys and games, and food. Involve everyone in the planning, so the anticipation will build.

54 *Try a family outing program.* If planning your own camping trip sounds overwhelming, check out the family outing programs offered by many local and state or provincial parks. Just go to your local or state/ provincial park Web sites and search for "family out- ings," "events," or "activities." Or give them a call. These programs last a night or two and usually are open to whoever wants to come. Guests stay in cabins and enjoy a variety of nature programs—and food is provided. Average cost ranges from $15 to $45 per night. Or consider the many programs available for teens and preteens through good public park systems, including junior ranger and junior naturalist programs. Other organizations, such as the Sierra Club's Build- ing Bridges to the Outdoors (www.sierraclub.org/ youth), also provide excellent youth nature programs.

55 *Find a great camp for your kids.* Camp can be a great place for kids to learn independence while experienc- ing nature firsthand. Camping experiences come in many varieties: day camp and overnight, weekend and monthlong, low-cost and high. Many camps offer scholarships and financial assistance. To be sure to send your kids to a camp that's right for them—and you—find out all you can about camps before signing up. Some questions to keep in mind: What activities does your child enjoy? What is the ratio of staff to campers? How much emphasis is placed on nature and opportunities for independent exploration of the environment? What food is served? Is the camp accredited by the state or province? A good place to start your search is The American Camp Association (www.campparents.org), which offers a guide and online database of more than 2,400 accredited camps in the United States, or CampResource.com, a similar resource for camps in the United States, Canada, and other countries.

56 *Volunteer at a public park.* This could be at a local park or botanical garden that needs extra help to keep it in good shape. Volunteers do any number of things, including removing ivy, rebuilding trails, planting seeds, or painting picnic tables. Or you could sign up for one of many cleanup operations such as the Adopt-a-Crag events organized by the Access Fund (www.accessfund .com) throughout the year. Go online and find out where the next event is happening in your area.

57 *Take a volunteer vacation.* If you're willing to volunteer your time, there are lots of inexpensive opportunities to vacation in comfort—surrounded by spectacular scenery. Just do an Internet search for "volunteer vacation" and explore the results until you find something that matches your needs. For example, Earthwatch Institute (www.earthwatch.org) offers opportunities for groups to help out on scientific expeditions, like studying whales in British Columbia or helping manage a rain forest in Puerto Rico. Also, lots of resorts, camps, and campgrounds have cleanup opportunities at the beginning and end of the camping season. These typically offer free or reduced lodging in exchange for a few hours work each day.

58 *Visit a cave or cavern.* Numerous national parks throughout North America feature spectacular natural caves and caverns, and many offer educational guided

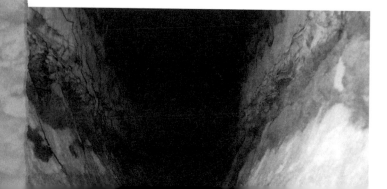

tours. You and your kids can learn about the living things perfectly suited to live inside of caves, such as crustaceans, mollusks, bats—even blind cave fish!—and plant life such as fungi, mosses, and lichen. You'll learn about the history of the caves, which may be hundreds of millions of years old, and you may even see fossils.

59 Participate in Wildlife Watch.
National Wildlife Federation's (NWF) Wildlife Watch Program is designed for nature-lovers of all ages. Your task is to let NWF know about the wildlife and plants you observe where you live. For example, when did you begin to see the fall foliage in your community? Have you noticed local wildlife preparing for winter? Does this autumn seem hotter or colder than past years? Go to the NWF site and report any interesting wildlife sightings in your neighborhood. Enter your postal code at www.naturefind.com/watch to get started; you'll be able to tell your story and share photos of your outdoor adventures. You can even share the latest on wildlife through Twitter, by putting "#nwf" in your tweets. When you record your observations, NWF and their Wildlife Watch partners collect and review your findings so they can track the health and behavior of wildlife and plant species.

60

Count the birds. Your kids can help scientists learn more about bird populations—like how factors such as weather and disease affect their numbers, and how migration patterns change over time. How? By counting birds in your area and submitting your results and observations. Among several programs are the Great Backyard Bird Count (www.birdcount.org) and the Bird Sleuth program at Cornell University (www.birds.cornell.edu/birdsleuth).

61

Watch those pigeons. Join Project PigeonWatch and help scientists solve the mystery of why pigeons come in so many colors. Kids can participate by observing and counting pigeons in their neighborhood. Go to www.pigeonwatch.org for free posters, a data sheet and return envelope, and a resource guide with instruction booklet.

Get Smart
Be Green Consumers—and Eaters!

One of the most powerful ways we can invest in Earth is through the decisions we make about how we spend our money. Being deliberate about the products we bring home, the food we consume, and the waste we produce not only can lead to a healthier planet, but also can improve our own physical and spiritual health. And when we model smart decisions for our children, we send a strong message to them, thus helping to build a better future, too.

Keep in mind, though, that none of us has to change the world on our own. Sometimes you may have to compromise. Ecologically sustainable products can be expensive, so choose what you can do . . . and do it. If you get a couple cloth totebags and use them for your grocery shopping, you're making a difference. Likewise, smaller changes may go

over better with kids. If your kids are used to eating fast food, for example, it may be difficult to completely ban it. Instead, arm them with information about the environmental and health costs associated with fast food and work out an agreement to reduce the number of fast-food meals you eat. Pick your battles wisely, focus on raising awareness, and keep a positive attitude. This chapter has 39 ways to be smarter consumers.

62 *Take kids shopping.* When shopping for your family or group, take the kids with you and let them help you make green decisions. Together, compare products and look for those that are the most environmentally responsible. For example, look at food labels and avoid products with chemical additives if possible. Look for labels such as *fair trade* and *organic.* For nonfood products, choose *natural* and *nontoxic* when possible. You'll find plenty of other ways to make green decisions in this chapter. You can also shop green online from sources such as Gaiam (www.gaiam.com), the Green Home (www.greenhome.com), and the Green Store (www.greenstore.com).

63 *Make thoughtful decisions.* Make a list before you go shopping, and stick to it once you get to the store. Resist impulse buys! Plan your lists together, so kids put analysis into the decisions, too. And if your kids want a toy or cool new gadget, urge them to consider it carefully before making the purchase. Ask: "Do you really need it? How much waste will it produce?"

64 *Think about packaging.* Help kids understand how much waste can be in packaging, especially in products with lots of individual containers, like juice boxes and single-serving yogurts. When you're choosing between two similar products, select the one with less packaging. That way, you won't be adding as much to the landfill. When packaging is necessary, seek out products with packaging that can be reused for other purposes at home, like a box that could be used to ship a package.

65 *Use recycled products.* Most of us recycle our cans and bottles, but that's only part of the recycling process. You can help complete the "cycle" in recycle by purchasing items made from recycled materials. Whether they are products made of paper, glass, wood, or even metal, take the recycled option and encourage your school, clubs, or any other organizations you're affiliated with to do the same. In the short term you may pay higher prices for some goods, but in the long term it will increase demand and thus lower prices. You can save money and help the planet if you avoid disposable items such as paper plates, plastic cups, and plastic utensils, in favor of the real things. You can also get biodegradable disposable products.

66 *Choose refillable.* Pens and mechanical pencils, laundry detergent, dish soap, toothpaste, and many other items are available in refillable containers, which produce much less waste than buying new containers each time. And although you may have to pay more for rechargeable batteries, in the long run they provide great savings. Be sure to involve your children in your purchases!

67 *Spend humanely.* Don't buy anything made of ivory, tortoise shell, coral, reptile skins, or exotic cat furs, all of which come from endangered animals or plants. Fewer people buying these items means it's harder for people to sell them. Lower demand will eventually lead to lower supply, which means fewer of these species will be hunted.

68 *Just say no to paper and plastic bags.* According to the Food Marketing Institute, the average consumer makes 1.9 trips to the grocery store each week. If you take home two paper grocery bags each trip, that's about 200 disposable bags a year. Even if you recycle your bags, it's better not to use them in the first place, due to the energy used to produce that bag. Instead, you and your kids can say no thanks when offered a bag at the grocery store, and carry your stuff home in a reusable tote bag.

69

Calculate the cost in trees. Sit with your kids for 30 minutes and watch people leaving the grocery store. Count all the paper bags you see going home with people. Next, figure out how long it will take this store to go through one whole tree. According to Energy Quest, a kid-friendly Web site of the California Energy Commission, a 15-year-old tree produces about 700 paper bags. Double the number of bags you saw in 30 minutes to give you a rough estimate of hourly bag consumption. Then, divide 700 by that number. For example, let's say you saw 40 bags leave your store. That's 80 bags an hour, so $700 \div 80 = 8.75$ hours per tree. These calculations are approximate, because traffic at the store is not consistent, but it helps kids understand the big picture.

70

CHECK OUT WHAT'S HAPPENING AROUND THE WORLD. _____

→ Like paper bags, plastic bags are bad for the earth, too, because they are made from petroleum and don't decompose. Some nations and cities are doing something about it. In Ireland, a steep fee introduced in 2003 has led people to use reusable cloth totes almost exclusively instead of plastic bags. China, Australia, South Africa, Switzerland, Germany, and the Netherlands have followed suit, and other nations are contemplating it as well. In the United States, San Francisco and Oakland have adopted similar policies, and many other cities are considering similar actions.

71

Clean up with vinegar. Clean surfaces in your home with a half-and-half solution of white distilled vinegar and water instead of detergents with polluting phosphorus. Because of its acidity, vinegar kills germs and bacteria as well as removes stains and odors. And, since water and vinegar are non-toxic, even your youngest kids can chip in to help (with some supervision, naturally). At about $3 a gallon, not only is it safer than store-bought cleansers, it's much less expensive. (Don't mix vinegar with other cleansers, though, as that may result in a dangerous chemical solution.)

72 *Choose durable clothing for your children.* Quality clothes don't need replacing as often, and you can pass them along in good condition when your kids outgrow them. Look for securely sewn buttons, tight stitching, and firm seams. Avoid clothes with bunched seams, lumpy stitching, sticky zippers, loose threads, wobbly buttons, and uneven or puckered hems. Check consumer Web sites or online retailers for customer feedback. You'll save money in the long run because you won't have to replace clothing as often, and you won't be contributing as much to the landfill.

73 *Know the fabric facts.* And teach them to your kids. When you shop together, look for items made of sustainable materials, such as hemp, bamboo, and organic wool and cotton. Organic clothing keeps harmful chemicals, fertilizers, and pesticides out of the ecosystem—and your child's body. More pesticides are used on cotton than on any other crop in the world, and they harm cotton workers, local wildlife, and your family, the consumers.

74

Use bamboo. Bamboo is the fastest growing plant on Earth, which makes it very sustainable (it can be harvested without being depleted or damaged). It also blocks dangerous UV rays and contains a unique antibacterial agent that is retained when it is made into fabric. As a result, bamboo products are odor resistant, stay fresher longer, and stop bacteria from spreading—better for your children's health! By contrast, some human-made chemical antibacterial fabrics can cause skin problems such as irritations or abrasions, particularly for people with sensitive or allergy-prone skin. Bamboo is also better for the environment, since it is 100 percent naturally grown, without assistance from people.

75 *Donate and purchase used clothes.* Together with your kids, gather up old clothes to pass on to a friend or donate to a local thrift store, Salvation Army, or Goodwill. This is a good way to involve kids as part of the solution, not only to reducing landfill but also to using resources well and helping others. Check out your local thrift store for yourself and your kids, too. Recycled clothes are both economical and environmentally friendly.

76 *Look for domestically produced clothing.* The raw materials for most clothing are grown (or manufactured), assembled, and packaged in separate countries, so the shipping to put them together produces tons of pollution. Look for labels stating items were produced in your country. Buying local reduces travel emissions.

77 *Take a toilet paper survey.* Help the environment by switching from colored to white toilet paper and buying toilet paper that is unscented, packaged in paper rather than plastic, and made from recycled paper. Some of the dyes and scents used on toilet paper produce toxins, substances that are poisonous to the environment when these papers decompose. According to the National Resources Defense Council, if every household in the United States replaced just one roll of virgin fiber toilet paper (500 sheets) with a 100 percent recycled roll, 423,900 trees would be saved. Have your kids conduct their own survey at the supermarket, checking five brands of paper for these factors, and deciding which brand is best for the environment.

If every household in the United States replaced just one roll of virgin fiber toilet paper (500 sheets) with a 100 percent recycled roll, 423,900 trees would be saved.

78

Buy in bulk. After you finish that toilet paper survey, buy the 24-pack instead of the 4-pack. If you're feeding a pet, buy the largest bag of food you can afford. Buy a jug of juice instead of juice boxes. Whenever possible, purchase as many of the items on your list in bulk form—large quantities without individual packaging— to save money and reduce the amount of packaging involved. A cautionary note, though: don't buy more than you will use. That just leads to more waste.

79 *Put a cap on bottled water.*
Americans will buy about 25 billion
single-serving plastic bottles of water
this year, according to the Container Recycling
Institute. Sure, bottled water is better for your kids
than pop or corn-syrupy juice boxes. But producing all
those bottles requires more than 1.5 billion barrels of
oil every year—enough to fuel about 100,000 cars for
the entire year. Worse yet, nearly 80 percent of those
bottles will end up in a landfill. And, according to the
Natural Resources Defense Council, 40 percent of
bottled water is nothing more than tap water anyway.
Tap water is more highly regulated than bottled water,
and it's virtually free. You can still have water on the
go with refillable water bottles for yourself and kids.

80 *Snip six-pack rings.* If your drinks
come in six packs, don't throw those
six-pack rings straight into the garbage.
Get your youngsters to snip each circle with scissors first.
Why? Many of these rings end up in oceans, lakes, and rivers, because they are left on the beach or in garbage dumps
near the water. Once they're in the water, they are invisible
to sea creatures and birds that may get caught up in them
while hunting for food. These animals can be hurt or even
killed as a result. But once the rings are cut, no animal

can get caught on them. Better yet, purchase drinks that are not packaged in six-pack rings. Discuss this with your kids: What's a better way to provide drinks for your group?

81 *Buy locally produced food.* When you do, you are helping reduce the pollution and depletion of resources associated with the transportation and packaging of food. On average, domestically grown produce sold in conventional supermarkets has traveled some 1,500 miles from farm to table. Not only that, it has probably been picked before it ripened and treated—possibly with fungicides—so it can travel and be stored. Locally grown, farm-fresh fruits and vegetables are typically picked at their peak, making for delicious, ready-to-eat produce. Go to www.localharvest .org to search by city, state, province, or postal code for farmers markets, grocery stores, and restaurants that sell food from your region.

82 *Frequent farmers markets.* These are great places to find local produce as well as other locally produced goods, including (at some farmers markets) garden plants, clothing, and arts and crafts. Many farmers markets have festive atmospheres, with live music as well as drinks and prepared foods available. Farmers markets can be a great way to get kids excited about buying local.

83

Go organic. When we're talking about raising a healthy generation of children, the less exposure to pesticides, hormones, and additives, the better. That's why it makes sense to buy organic products, especially produce. Though this can be expensive, you can save money by prioritizing produce that contains the most pesticides, including peaches, apples, bell peppers, celery, nectarines, cherries, lettuce, imported grapes, pears, spinach, and potatoes. Of course, chemicals also negatively affect the environment and the people who work the fields. As consumer demand shifts from conventional produce to organic, more companies may go organic, so your purchasing decisions can help the environment and help keep workers healthier, too.

Save money by prioritizing produce that contains the most pesticides, including peaches, apples, bell peppers, celery, nectarines, cherries, lettuce, imported grapes, pears, spinach, and potatoes.

---

84 *Go even more organic.* Purchase organic canned foods and other products whenever possible. They're not much more expensive, and you'll send a powerful message to the food industry as well as to your children.

85 *Learn your labels.*

100% USDA Organic Certified Foods. This label tells consumers that the organic foods they are purchasing have been produced and processed in accordance with national organic standards set by the U.S. Department of Agriculture. It applies to fresh, raw products, as well as to processed products that contain organic agricultural ingredients. Only food labeled "100% Organic" is totally organic, while food labeled "Organic" is 95 percent organic.

FTC: Fair Trade Certified. May apply to food or clothing. It lets you know that the farmers and farm workers in developing nations have received a fair price for their product—also that they encourage sustainable farming methods, limit the use of pesticides, and do not use forced child labor.

Leaping Bunny. Found on cleaning products and personal hygiene products. This tells you that the company making this product adheres to the Corporate Standard of Compassion for Animals, basically a pledge not to conduct or commission testing of their products on animals.

FSC: Forest Stewardship Council Certified. Found on paper products and wood, a product with this label has been certified by the FSC to meet their standards, guaranteeing that the wood has been harvested from a well-managed forest. The FSC has 10 specific principles of management, covering the environmental, social, and economic impact of the forest industry.

Energy Star. Look for this symbol on appliances, heating and cooling systems, even entire homes. Products with this label meet the strict energy efficiency guidelines set by Energy Star, an international program first created by the U.S. Environmental Protection Agency (EPA); they use less energy and less water than comparable products.

86 *Watch your fish.* Fishing practices worldwide are damaging our oceans—depleting fish populations, destroying habitats, and polluting the water. As an informed consumer, you can help turn the tide. By choosing fish that are abundant, well-managed, and caught or farmed in environmentally friendly ways, you and your family can support fisheries and fish farms that are healthier for ocean wildlife and the environment. Ask your fishmonger for help choosing, or check out the Monterey Bay Aquarium's free downloadable pocket guides, at www.mbayaq.org (click on Seafood Watch).

87 *Limit your tuna consumption.* Tuna is a good source of omega-3 fatty acids, which reduce the risk of heart attack by one-third in adults and are good for kids, too. But fishing practices used by the global tuna industry are contributing to the sharp decline of populations of sea turtles, sharks, rays, and other marine animals. For example, long-line fishing involves trailing a single line with hundreds or thousands of hooks. The World Wildlife Federation (WWF) estimates that up to 13,500 seabirds, including 10,000 albatrosses—most species of which are endangered—are caught in these hooks every year. A healthy diet includes seafood about twice a week, but mix in salmon, shellfish, and other options to reduce the amount of tuna you consume.

88 *Cut down on beef consumption.*
The United Nations Food and Agriculture Organization has estimated that direct emissions from meat production account for about 18 percent of the world's total greenhouse gas emissions. Producing a pound of beef requires 30 times more water than producing a pound of wheat and 200 times more than a pound of potatoes. According to a report produced by the World Wildlife Fund, more pasture is used for cattle than all other domesticated animals and crops combined. The average American eats roughly four servings of beef each week—cutting out even just one of them would help.

89 *Go vegetarian once a week.*
A vegetarian diet is better for the environment: global warming, over-exploited natural resources, deforestation, and water and air pollution are all directly linked to eating meat. So why not fight climate change with diet change, and go veggie? Meat lovers don't have to quit, but eating vegetarian one day a week, or one *more* day a week, would make a difference. You don't have to get too

exotic: think grilled cheese sandwiches or pasta with marinara sauce to get started.

90 *Make your own.* Even if you need food in a hurry, making it at home will almost always be cheaper and healthier than eating out. How long can it take to assemble a peanut butter and jelly sandwich with celery and carrot sticks on the side, or to pull out some salad ingredients and toss them together? You'll save the packaging and waste and know exactly what's in your food—no secret additives for you!

91 *Keep it interesting.* Check out some of the many online options for healthy, green recipes. At Care2's Healthy and Green Living page (www.care2.com/greenliving/food -recipes), you'll find plenty of choices, updated daily. A recent selection included Irish stew, baked apple-cinnamon French toast, and savory carrot tart.

92 *If you eat out, choose a green restaurant.* If you take your kids out to eat, patronize restaurants that use local and organic foods. Ask at your favorite restaurant or search by postal code at the Eat Well Guide (www.eatwellguide.com) for a list of restaurants that do.

93 CHECK OUT WHAT'S HAPPENING AROUND THE WORLD.

→ Slow Food is an international organization founded in 1989 "to counteract fast food and fast life, the disappearance of local food traditions and people's dwindling interest in the food they eat, where it comes from, how it tastes and how our food choices affect the rest of the world." Through taste education, the organization helps people learn about food in order to enjoy it more. According to the group's Web site, www.slowfood.com, "Slow Food is good, clean, and fair food." The organization has more than 100,000 members in 132 countries.

94 *Reduce food waste.* Get in the habit of serving smaller portions, and tell kids they can come back for more if they're still hungry. This can help you cut down on the amount of food you throw out, shrink your grocery bills, and slim down everybody's waistline!

95 *Choose cloth napkins.* It's a simple fact: cloth napkins are reusable and don't contribute to landfills. When they get dirty, you can wash them and use them again instead of throwing them in the garbage like paper napkins. Since napkins are small and easily tossed in with your other laundry, no additional resources are required to launder them. To help encourage the right spirit, have your kids create napkin rings for everyone in your family and decorate each ring uniquely.

96 *Stamp out Styrofoam.* Not long ago, no one thought twice about drinking out of a Styrofoam cup and tossing it in the trash. Now we know that Styrofoam doesn't decompose—50 or more years from now, a child might be digging in his backyard and find a chunk of a foam cup that was used today. Styrofoam also contains chlorofluorocarbons (CFCs), which are damaging to the environment. In 2006, the city of Santa Monica, California, took the bold step of banning Styrofoam in its eating establishments, and plenty of institutions have since followed suit. What can you do? Aside from simply not purchasing Styrofoam products, ask for paper cups and plates when eating at take-out or fast-food restaurants. If the restaurant only has Styrofoam, don't patronize it—and explain why you're not. If companies know they may lose business, they'll listen.

97

Have a living Christmas tree. If you celebrate Christmas and usually buy or cut down a fresh tree every year, consider getting a living Christmas tree this year. After the holidays, you can plant it in the ground or keep it in its pot and use it again next year. You can even donate it to a plant-a-tree organization. Living trees are becoming a popular choice for environmentally-conscious Christmas celebrators.

98 ***Do "The Compact."*** In December 2005, a group of friends in San Francisco made an agreement, or compact, to go one year without buying anything new except food and health and safety items (though they could purchase secondhand products). Their goal was to help preserve the environment by reducing the number of new products brought into it, as well as to simplify their lives. Since then, people around the world have taken up the idea. It's a great way to challenge yourself to do more for the planet, and to become more aware of what you consume. Try the Compact for one month your first time—and if you like the way that feels, go longer the next time.

99 ***Leave the car at home.*** One simple way to be a smarter consumer is to leave the car at home next time you go to the store. In 2008, 245 million vehicles were on the road in the United States—more than any other country—and 20.5 million in Canada. All that car exhaust adds to the greenhouse effect, acid rain, and smog. If every family chose to bike or bus for shopping trips—at least sometimes—it could make a big difference.

Get Active
More than Just the 3 Rs

Some of us remember when recycling meant loading up the car with yucky cans and bottles and driving to the one place in town that could handle our reusables. Thankfully, times have changed: Many cities have curbside pickup, and many public buildings have bins set out for easy use. Recycling is one of the most important things we can do to preserve our planet, and it includes not only recycling cans and bottles, but purchasing products made from recycled materials whenever possible.

Recycling is actually the third—and last—of the "3 Rs": *reduce, reuse, recycle*. Together these three words make up the most effective way to cut down on the amount of waste we produce. According to the Environmental Protection

Agency, the amount of waste each person creates has almost doubled since 1960, from 2.7 to 4.6 pounds per day. To help improve things, we can *reduce* our waste by purchasing less in the first place. We can find ways to *reuse* things we purchase, which delays or even prevents it from ending up in a landfill. These practices conserve money and resources and reduce pollution. Though recycling is far better for the planet than regular garbage, it still uses resources and causes pollution. Reducing and reusing should be our first priorities.

This chapter has 33 things you and your kids can do—beyond setting your recycling on the curb each week—to make the 3 Rs an active, hands-on experience for everyone.

100 *Donate or consign used items.* The clothes, toys, and bicycles your child has outgrown, for example, can be resold in a consignment shop or given to a charity to be used by someone else. Charity shops accept all sorts of used items, including clothing, shoes, small and large electronic appliances, sports equipment, computers, CDs, and DVDs. You can make a little cash or support your favorite charity and reduce the amount of waste going into landfills at the same time. But be sure to call ahead because the Consumer Product Safety Commission (in the United States) has set standards for testing the lead content of children's products. A resale store may not be accepting some items.

101 *Freecycle.* After spring cleaning, keep items out of the landfill with a stoop or garage sale, or by "Freecycling," with the help of a network of over 6 million people worldwide who are dedicated to connecting stuff with people who can use it. Check them out at www.freecycle.org.

102 *Make art.* What once was garbage now has artistic possibilities. See what you and your kids can make with bottle caps, old wrappers, ribbons, bows, milk cartons, and toilet paper rolls. Reuse old paper to make papier-mâché. With an old shoe box and scraps of unwanted fabric, you can create a crazy quilt box. An old T-shirt can become a child's art smock.

103 *Exchange toys.* Instead of buying new toys, set up a toy exchange with friends or neighbors. Swap a boxful of your child's old toys with a boxful of toys from a friend's home, and keep rotating them. Make sure the kids agree on what to trade! You can also exchange books, movies, and music, or check out your local library to borrow these.

104 *Brush up on recycling knowledge.* Policy changes, so go online to check out what your city recycles, how it should be sorted, how to get recycling containers, and how often recycling is picked up. (You might be surprised at what can be recycled!) Post the guidelines near your recycling bins for the whole family to see.

105 *Know the top 10.* According to the National Recycling Coalition (www.nrc-recycle.org), these are the top 10 most important items to recycle: aluminum, PET plastic bottles (polyethylene terephthalate, usually used for carbonated drinks and water bottles), news-paper, corrugated cardboard, steel cans, HDPE plastic bottles (high-density polyethylene, used for detergents, bleach, shampoo, milk jugs, and other purposes), glass containers, magazines, mixed paper, and computers.

106 *Model your commitment to the 3 Rs.* When you're pressed for time, it may be tempting to toss that empty soup can in the trash rather than clean it out and recycle it. But let's face it, one can is one too many—and if you don't set a good example for your kids, who are they going to learn from? Ask kids to help out with collecting and sorting. Talk with them about how recycling preserves natural resources, reduces greenhouse-gas emissions, creates jobs, saves energy, and keeps toxins from leaking out of landfills.

107 *Reuse your shoes.* Some big companies are coming up with exciting ways to reduce, reuse, and recycle. One such idea is Nike's Reuse-A-Shoe program. Get your school or youth group to collect old athletic shoes, and Nike will grind them up and use the rubber to make sports surfaces for running tracks, soccer fields, basketball courts, and playgrounds. Kids will enjoy imagining their shoes making this metamorphosis. Check out the program at www.nikereuseashoe.com.

108

Weigh your waste. Try this experiment with your children: weigh on a bathroom scale every bag of garbage you create before you take it out. Do it for a whole week, and multiply that total by 52 to get a rough estimate of how much waste you produce in a year. Then, as a group, make a goal of cutting your waste production by a pound a week. Where can you cut back to make that happen? Change your buying habits or start composting organic waste? Make a plan, then record your results for a week. Did your trash slim down by a pound? If not, figure out what else you can do. Fifty-two pounds a year is a real difference!

Make a goal of cutting your waste production by a pound a week. Where can you cut back to make that happen?

109

Create an energy contract. Together with your children, think of three things each of you can do to conserve energy during a two-week period. Make them three things you don't already do—or don't do well enough—and then write a contract promising to do these three things. They don't have to be huge things.

Here are some ideas: walk or ride a bike to school; turn off all electronics, like computers, televisions, stereos, and video games, when you leave a room; spend less time on computers or video games; use a manual pencil sharpener instead of an electric one; take shorter showers. If you want, build an award into the contract for sticking with it for two weeks, such as a family pizza night.

110 *Avoid the "Print" button.* Think twice before printing from the computer. You can read most documents and magazines online, and you can pay many bills via the Web, too. Kids can make or select e-cards for birthdays and other celebrations to save both paper and cash. When you must print, use both sides of a piece of paper whenever possible, and use recycled printer paper.

111 *Adjust your window shades.* Drapes or blinds can make a big difference in your home's heat. Open them up on sunny winter days to let the sun shine into your home, then close them at night to reduce heat loss. During the summer, keep the window coverings closed over sunny windows to reduce heat from the sun. If you live in a warm climate, add an insulating lining to your drapes to prevent the sun from overheating your home.

112

Attack the energy monster!
Everyone should turn off the lights when they leave a room, but sometimes it's hard to remember. To help keep the light switch in people's minds, post small, fun, homemade signs by the most-used ones. Draw an energy monster or an electricity vampire (time to get creative!) ready to devour your home, with the reminder: "Turn me off—bwa ha ha!" You can also conserve energy by replacing your incandescent bulbs with compact fluorescent light bulbs (CFLs) and by using the minimum amount of outdoor security lights—set them on a timer or motion sensor so they turn off during the day.

113 *Watch that water.* Turning off the water while you brush your teeth will save four gallons a minute. In the shower, turning off the water while you shampoo and condition your hair can save more than 50 gallons a week. Short showers use less hot water than baths, and low-flow showerheads—though they cost a few dollars to convert to—lead to big water savings over time. Talk with kids about other ways you can save water. If you make it a team effort, you can save plenty of water.

114 *Shoot for shorter showers.* Here's a way kids and adults can cut down shower times. First, time your shower using a clock or timer. Next, find out how much water you used by holding a bucket under the showerhead for 30 seconds, then measuring the contents of the bucket with a measuring cup. Convert your shower time to seconds (as opposed to minutes and seconds), divide the total seconds by 30, and multiply that number by the number of cups you got in 30 seconds. That's how much water you use every time you shower. Now you can calculate how much water your showers use yearly and set a goal to reduce that usage by 10 percent. So if you use 2,275 gallons of water a year, you can save 227 gallons a year by shaving 10 percent from your daily shower time. If you take six-minute showers (360 seconds), that means cutting only 36 seconds—a small change for a huge annual difference!

115 *Charge up without using electricity.* If you or your kids are permanently plugged into a laptop, video game, PDA, or MP3 player, consider a solar-powered battery charger. They're small enough to fit in a backpack, and most models are compatible with just about any device. How cool to power your electronics directly from the sun! You can find models at Sundance Solar (http://store.sundancesolarcorp.com), Solio (www.solio.com), and Solar Style (www.solarstyle.com).

116 *Become a leak-seeker.* Even a tiny leak can waste a lot of water. For example, a leak that fills a coffee cup in 10 minutes will waste more than 3,000 gallons of water in a year. Here's one way to seek leaks: show your child how to read the water meter. She can read the meter and write down what it says at a time when everyone is out of the house or won't be using water. An hour later, have her take another reading. If the numbers have changed, she's found a leak. Time to get to work! First check individual water systems like toilets, sprinkler systems, and water softeners. If you still haven't found the problem, try checking the main service line. You can do this by closing the water shutoff valve to your home, turning on a faucet inside to check that there is no water flowing inside, and then check the meter. If it's still moving, the leak most likely is between the shutoff valve and the water meter.

117 **Don't let it drip.** It's easy to detect leaks in your toilets. Put about 12 drops of red or blue food coloring in the tank, wait about 15 minutes (be sure to guard the door, so no one uses the toilet while you're waiting), and look in the toilet bowl. If you see colored water, your tank is leaking.

118 **Use less water, flush by flush.** Most toilets use more water than they need to: about four gallons every time you flush. Under the supervision of an adult, help your kids save water by putting something in each toilet tank in your home, school, or other building to take up space, so the toilet will use less water. Put small rocks in a plastic container to make it heavier, fill it with water, and put the cap on. Now put the container in the toilet tank, taking care that it doesn't get in the way of the arm or chain that helps the toilet flush. You'll save between one and two gallons of water every time someone flushes that toilet. A note of caution: Experts advise against putting a brick in your tank, since bricks can break down and clog the pipes. You can also install a low-flow toilet, which uses only around 1.6 gallons per flush. Save even more water with a dual-flusher, a toilet with two flushing options: less water for number one, more water for number two.

119 *Pack waste-free lunches.* According to www.wastefreelunches.org, each school-age child who packs a disposable lunch (a lunch whose contents are packed in single-use plastic bags, aluminum foil, or wax paper, or that contains single-serving items that come in disposable packages) generates 67 pounds of waste per school year. That works out to 18,760 pounds of lunch waste for just one average-size elementary school—a mountain of trash. Pack a waste-free lunch for everyone in your family, and you'll be doing your part to reduce the mountain. Opt for reusable sandwich containers, cloth napkins, metal forks and spoons, reusable drink containers, and reusable lunch boxes or bags. You can also talk to kids about what they really eat when they get to school, and agree on items they won't end up throwing away—and therefore wasting.

120

Create a green team. Your kids can conduct an environmental survey in your home, school, youth group, or place of worship, and brainstorm ways to make improvements. They can assess the level of waste and check the building for inefficiencies such as leaky faucets or electric equipment left on overnight. Eco-savvy green team members can initiate a recycling program, present environmental workshops, or lobby to replace existing light bulbs with energy-saving compact fluorescents (CFLs). Or consider LED (light-emitting diode) lighting as well, an even greener lighting option. Imagine this: LED bulbs last up to 20 years. Examples of environmental surveys and audit tools can be found in the resources section of Green Schools (www.greenschools.net), under Curricula.

121 *Behold the power of power strips.* Even when appliances are off, they still drain energy in "standby" mode. One solution is to plug these appliances into power strips. You and your kids can easily get in the habit of using the strips to turn off televisions, stereos, and computers when not using them. Or go one better and get a Smart Power Strip. It works like this: one "Control Outlet" controls six other outlets on the strip. If you plug a computer (or something else) into the Control Outlet, the other outlets on the strip will automatically shut off when you turn off the computer (or put it to "sleep"). There are also three other outlets that are "always on."

122 *Beat the heat—and the AC—by degrees.* Include your kids in decisions about the temperature in your home or building. During summer months, agree to bump up the thermostat higher than you normally do if you have air conditioning, and open the windows when there is a breeze. Bump it down a notch in the winter. If you normally keep the thermostat at 69, agree to try 68 for a few days and see how that feels. If everyone is comfortable, drop it down to 67. When you're sleeping or not in the building, turn it down even more. According to Energy Star, a U.S. government program dedicated to protecting the environment through energy efficient practices, you can save up to 30 percent of your current utility bill just by making more efficient choices. So if your annual heating bill is around $2,000, your family could end up with an extra $600—and you trim your carbon emissions!

123 *Be draft detectives.* Conserving energy also means checking for cracks around windows and doors, since these are big energy wasters. On the next cold, windy day, give your child a piece of ribbon or light paper to hold near all your windowsills and outside door jambs. If the ribbon or paper flutters, she's found a leak. Check for broken weather-stripping seals or chipped or missing glazing (the putty that holds the glass in the frame).

124 *Organize an eco-friendly fund-raiser.* Does your group need to raise money? Maybe you need to make those green upgrades such as installing low-flow showerheads or toilets or initiating a recycling program. You don't necessarily have to sell anything to raise money. Instead, put together a walk-a-thon, obstacle course, or marathon dancing contest and raise money through donations for every lap walked, obstacle achieved, or hour danced. That way, kids get exercise, your school or club makes money, no new products (or waste!) are added to the environment, and everyone has fun. For more options, check out Greenraising (www .greenraising.com) and Let'sGoGreen (www.letsgogreen .biz), just two of the organizations that offer opportunities to raise money without trashing the planet. Another great green option is to sell reusable grocery bags through companies such as ChicoBag (www.chicobag .com) or ReuseThisBag (www.reusethisbag.com).

125

Green your students' curriculum. As a teacher or a parent, you can talk to school officials about adding environmental issues to the curriculum. Environmental education is easily incorporated into science classes, but it can also be integrated into math lessons, reading assignments, service learning projects, and creative art activities. Take some time to find out who has the most sympathetic ear at your child's school, and start there. Come prepared with facts: Research shows that a green curriculum is good for the planet and for our children's character, and it's also good for children's intellects, emotional lives, and imagination. Be sure to take a positive approach, show enthusiasm, and be ready to volunteer your help.

126

CHECK OUT WHAT'S HAPPENING AROUND THE WORLD.

→ The Eco-Schools program has been adopted by more than 21,000 schools in 44 countries. The program teaches kids about sustainable development by encouraging them to take an active role in how their school can be run in a more eco-friendly way. It is sponsored by the Foundation for Environmental Education (FEE), a program of the United Nations. Learn more at www.eco-schools.org.

127

Have a can-do attitude.

Recycling cans is super efficient! Recycling just one saves enough energy to power your TV for three hours. Making cans from recycled aluminum uses 95 percent less energy than making cans from raw materials. Aluminum cans are the most recycled beverage container in the world—but we can do better! Place a bin next to your school or club's vending machine to collect empty cans, carry a bag to collect cans after the kids' sports events, and, when you have the choice between plastic bottles or aluminum cans, choose aluminum.

128

Create a compost pile. Compost will turn your yard waste and kitchen scraps into mulch you can use to feed your plants. For a successful compost pile, you need both *brown materials,* which are good sources of carbon—shredded newspapers (but no colored paper), cardboard, straw, yard waste, and dried leaves—and *green materials,* good sources of nitrogen—food scraps, vegetable and fruit waste, coffee grounds, eggshells, and lawn clippings. Aim for a ratio of roughly 4 parts brown to 1 part green. Don't include meat scraps, bones, or cheese, since these are slow to break down and attract animals. Also avoid food with artificial ingredients, diseased plants, dog or cat feces, and treated logs. Organic material needs water to decompose, so add water as needed to keep it moist but not too wet, and turn the pile periodically. This adds oxygen and promotes decay of the contents. Let kids help with this; it's icky and fun. Many cities either offer free construction materials or the option of purchasing a bin at reduced cost. Check your city's Web site for more information. To learn more about composting, do an Internet search for "composting instructions."

129

Bring home some worms.

Vermi-composting is an excellent way to learn about ecology while turning your food scraps into usable compost. Build or buy a wooden box about two feet by two feet and eight inches deep, and make drain holes near the bottom. Fill the box with moist bedding. This can be shredded paper or newspaper, leaves, straw, peat moss, or sawdust. Be sure to keep it moist like a sponge and change it once or twice a year. Now buy some red worms and put them in. It's important to get red wrigglers or red earthworms and not nightcrawlers, which are not good composters. Add one pound of worms for every half pound of food to start. They will multiply quickly! Put in two handfuls of soil. Mix in household garbage such as fruit, vegetables, coffee grounds, bread, and leaves (but *not* milk, oil, eggs, meat fat, dog or cat feces), and stand back; the worms will eat the rotting garbage and make soil—some of the finest, most fertile soil around.

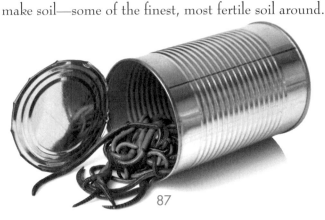

130

CHECK OUT WHAT'S HAPPENING AROUND THE WORLD.

→ Vermicomposting is international. An organization in India has helped more than 2,000 farmers and institutions switch from conventional chemicals to vermicompost. It has also developed methods to convert biodegradable industrial waste like pulp waste from paper mills into vermicompost. Three facilities are producing 30 tons of vermicompost each month from this type of waste. Cuba, with reduced availability of imported fossil fuels, pesticides, and fertilizers, has made worms a key to their agriculture. Japan has three 1,000-ton-per-month facilities that vermicompost the wastes from pulp and food processing companies. The sale of vermicompost and fish bait helps pay for these operations. Vancouver, British Columbia's Office of Urban Agriculture subsidizes worm bin kits and even provides workshops at the Vancouver Compost Demonstration Garden.

131

Try grasscycling. Bagging up yard trimmings after you cut the grass wastes your time and energy. It also puts a tremendous strain on the environment when those bags end up in a landfill. Instead, try grasscycling. Leave grass clippings on your lawn where they will naturally decompose and hold in soil moisture, prevent freezing, and return nutrients to the soil. However, it's important that your grass is not too long, or the clippings can harm your lawn. For best results, your grass should be dry, the mower blades should be sharp, and you should not be cutting more than one third of the length of the grass blade at one time. During a wet season, or a time when you can't mow as frequently as necessary, your grass might be longer. This is an excellent opportunity to rake up your clippings and add them to a compost pile.

132 Mulch—it goes a long way.

With your children, mulch around your trees, shrubs, and flower beds to help control weeds (thus saving the need for pesticides), maintain more consistent soil temperature, and keep the soil moist, which reduces the need for constant watering. You can buy mulch, or you can make your own by shredding leaves, sticks, grass, bark, compost, and other organic material. Besides the benefits to your yard, mulching is a kind of recycling and saves the environment from more landfill.

Get Involved
Take a Green Stand

When kids get involved in a cause, they can make a real difference. Consider Haruka Maruno, a Japanese girl who invented a tool for scooping dog poop that would decompose in landfills—unlike the plastic bags people usually use. Or Henry Cilley of Chicago, who saved the habitat of endangered turtles in his neighborhood by collecting more than 700 signatures on a petition and convincing a construction company to build accommodations for the turtles into its construction plans.

Tell your kids about these examples, and look for others, too (a good place to start is www.myhero .com; click on "Heroes"). Be inspired. Then be a role model for your kids by joining them to support a cause you all feel strongly about, whether it's big or small—sometimes a small start can lead to much bigger things. This chapter has 18 ways to join forces with your kids and take a green stand.

133 *Find your cause.* Being an activist for the planet means deciding what it is you feel strongly about. Get informed about environmental issues by regularly reading the Local section of your area's newspaper or subscribing to a quality environmental magazine such as *E—The Environmental Magazine*, *National Geographic*, or *Orion Magazine*. Or check out www.idealist.org to find suggestions for ways you can make a difference in your own neighborhood. Still unsure? Go to www.care2 .com, the Web site for Care2, an organization whose mission is to help people preserve the environment by connecting them with individuals, organizations, and responsible businesses making an impact. You'll find hundreds of different causes to choose from. Find one that grabs you.

134 *Learn all you can.* Once you have settled on a cause to embrace, gather all the information you can. If it's a local issue that attracts you, such as the health of a stream or lake, start with your city's Web site, check with National and State or Provincial Park Services, or ask a librarian (also known as a media specialist) for help. For a national issue, you can probably do most of your research online. Explore all sides of the issue and delegate members of the family or group to research the various organizations involved. The more you know, the better prepared you are to do something.

135 Find strength in numbers.

Join an environmental group with your kids and support the efforts of thousands of like-minded activists. Options include the Sierra Club (www.sierraclub.org), the Environmental Defense Fund (www.edf.org), the Natural Resources Defense Council (www.nrdc.org), and the Humane Society (www.hsus.org). By signing up with the Sierra Club, for example, you'll be standing alongside 1.3 million other members, all working together to protect our communities and the planet. Once you join, you can support issues like stopping mountaintop-removal coal mining, protecting the wilderness, and standing up for smart solutions to invasive species. Sign petitions, write letters, visit your congressional representative; when you're working with thousands of volunteers, you can make a difference.

136 *Organize a cleanup day.* If you are tired of trash or vandalism in part of your neighborhood, why not organize a day to clean it up? Take a look around and decide where you want to start: a park filled with litter, a vacant lot where people have dumped old furniture, a public wall that's been tagged? Ask permission from the private owner or government agency responsible for the property. You can do your cleanup day with just a few kids, or you can take it a step further. To have the best effect, ask a lot of people to participate—and then ask more. Consider inviting scouts, campfire groups, and religious groups. Hold a planning meeting, agree on a time and place, and get the supplies you'll need—trash bags, gloves, graffiti remover, prizes for people who pick up the most garbage, and so on. To raise awareness, send a press release to local papers, community calendars, and online groups. Post flyers in laundromats, YMCAs, and wherever people gather. Finally, on the big day, hang a big sign, kick off your event, find tasks for everyone, and be sure to thank all the participants. Celebrate what you've been able to do together!

137

Raise litter awareness. Model litter responsibility by taking a trash bag with you on hikes or walks to accommodate your own trash as well as the trash you find. Whenever you're out, remind youngsters to throw their garbage in trash cans—and their recyclables in recycling bins, when available, or take them home to recycle—and encourage them to take care of other people's litter when they see it. Take litter-consciousness one step further by organizing a "Litter Drive" at your school or youth group. See how many pieces of litter kids can collect in a school yard, park, or playground in your town.

138 *Jump start recycling in your community.* If your local utilities haven't caught up with recycling yet, you can organize your own recycling effort. Ask friends and neighbors to put out their cans and bottles on a specific day and let you pick them up and haul them to the recycling center. If this first wave is successful, expand your efforts to a wider swath of the community. You may even gain some allies to help you in your cause. This is also a great idea for a green fund-raiser, since you can probably make a few bucks from all those cans.

139 CHECK OUT WHAT'S HAPPENING AROUND THE WORLD.

→ When nine-year-old Savannah Walters of Odessa, Florida, learned that Americans waste 4 million gallons of gas each day by driving on under-inflated tires, she decided to do something about it. She adopted the catchy phrase "Pump 'Em Up" and started going door to door in her neighborhood with 99-cent tire gauges, showing adults how to get better fuel economy by putting the right amount of air in their tires. She has put up a Web site, www.pumpemup.org, lobbied Washington, spread her campaign to 10 states, and appeared on *NBC Nightly News with Brian Williams.*

140 *Defend an endangered species.* Due to habitat destruction and other environmental damage caused by humans, a huge number of species are endangered around the world. Have your kids go to Kids' Planet (www.kidsplanet.org), the World Wildlife Fund (www.worldwildlife.org), or the National Wildlife Federation (www.nwf.org), where they can learn about endangered animal species and choose one to help protect. After they choose a species, they can learn more about it, learn what to do to protect it, and get ideas for raising awareness about it. They can even adopt a wild animal. For example, you can symbolically adopt a desert tortoise from the NWF for $30, money that will be spent to protect one of Earth's oldest species.

141 *Protect a local species.* You also can contact your state or provincial fish and game or natural resources department to find out which animals that live in your area are endangered, what is being done to protect them, and how you can help. Start by finding contact info on their Web site.

142 *Celebrate successes.* Sign up for Endangered Species Day, the third Friday of every May, when thousands of families go to their local parks, wildlife refuges, zoos, aquariums, schools, and community centers to celebrate endangered species success stories (such as the American bald eagle) and help raise awareness about currently endangered species. You can take part in festivals, film showings, field trips, and park tours to learn about the importance of protecting endangered species and everyday actions you can take to help save local disappearing wildlife.

143 *Participate in an Earth Day event.* Designed to educate people about Earth's environment and ways to protect it, Earth Day is observed annually on April 22 by countries around the world. Earth Day events include fairs, festivals, educational talks, and hands-on activism like park restoration, tree planting, and river cleanups. Go to www.earthday.net and mouse over "Get Active" to find events and volunteer opportunities in your area. Join in to help keep our planet clean and healthy.

> *Earth Day events include fairs, festivals, educational talks, and hands-on activism like park restoration, tree planting, and river cleanups.*

144 *Help protect the rain forests.* It's estimated that about 100 acres of rain forests are cut down per minute, a rate that would eliminate all the rain forests of the world in just a few decades if allowed to continue. Although rain forests cover only a small part of Earth, they are home to more than half of the world's plants and animals. With your kids, visit the Rainforest Alliance Web site at www.rainforest-alliance.org to see how you can take action. Through their Adopt-A-Rainforest program, you can contribute funding to support the purchase and sustainable management of tropical rain forests. You'll get a certificate as a thank you, but you will also have access to numerous educational materials such as stories, lesson plans, and presentations—especially useful for teachers to connect their students with conservation projects. To increase your impact, put on a green fund-raiser (see page 83) to make a bigger donation.

145 Take your carbon footprint.
Calculate what you're contributing to global warming. The measure of a person's impact is often called a carbon footprint because carbon dioxide is the most common greenhouse gas. You can find carbon footprint calculators at www.earthlab.com/carbonprofile or www.zerofootprintoffsets.com, and in about three minutes you'll discover how your own actions and lifestyle impact the planet. One note of caution: since different carbon footprint calculators use different methods, your results may vary. But even if the measurements are not completely accurate, you can still use them to set goals to lower your carbon output—and to measure your success.

146 *Remodel your home the green way.* Okay, this is a big one. But if you're planning to make changes anyway, there are plenty of ways to remodel your home the green way. First, use renewable or recycled materials: bamboo flooring and recycled glass tiles are a good place to start. Use wood certified by the Forest Stewardship Council (FSC), which means it comes from forests that are managed to meet the social, economic, and ecological needs of present and future generations. A green roof (one that is partially or completely covered with soil and vegetation and planted over a waterproofing membrane) helps cool

your home in the summer, insulate it in the winter, absorb rainwater, and minimize runoff. Consider solar rooftop panels to generate your home's electricity, and create a system to use rainwater and "grey water" (rinse water from the clothes washer, shower, etc.) to flush toilets and replenish outdoor greenery. For more information—and to find a contractor who can help you with these changes—go to www.allgreencontractors.com.

147

Make news. Together with your kids, decide on an issue you care about and write a letter to a newspaper or Web site. To increase your chances of getting published, start your letter with a startling fact or a question: Did you know that the bottling process for bottled water consumes the energy equivalent of 17 million barrels of oil a year? Pack your letter with lots of facts. And if the first letter doesn't get published, keep writing. The more times you write, the better your chances that one of your letters will be published. The thrill of seeing your name in print, along with knowing that you are educating people about a topic you're passionate about, will be worth the work.

148 *Write to leaders.* Young people can get very passionate about their beliefs, and a powerful way to use that passion is to have them write to senators, congresspeople, and even world leaders about their concerns. Encourage your kids to stand up and speak out for our great planet Earth. Concerned that there aren't enough trees in your community? Write to city officials, asking that they form a tree committee. Are you seeing state, provincial, and local parks falling into disrepair? Write to your representatives or senators, demanding that they take action. Have you heard about people who have been imprisoned for working peacefully to try to prevent excessive logging in their country's forests? Take action by writing to that country's leader, demanding the release of these prisoners. Most leaders have email addresses, but sometimes a fax or a snail mail letter can be more effective.

149 *Be heard online.* It's easy to set up a blog or Web site that promotes an environmental cause that's important to you and your kids. Go to one of the popular blogging platforms such as blogger.com or blogspot.com and follow the simple instructions to set yourselves up. Many computers come with easy-to-use Web site applications, too. Since most kids find technology to be very cool, they'll get excited about transferring their eco-passion to an online setting—and chances are they'll be very good at it. Your site can include reporting on local issues that kids research themselves, interviews they conduct with environmentalists, and your own suggestions for how to help the cause. Many of your youngsters will know how to create podcasts, another interesting option. They can even get out into nature and report "on location from the field."

150

Network for a green cause. If your kids are teens, point them toward www.planet-connect.org. Planet Connect is a social networking site where teens can learn about environmental issues; get information about environmental clubs, activities, and volunteer opportunities; learn about environmental college programs, careers, and green jobs; socialize with like-minded teens; and be part of a green community. Planet Connect also offers a grant program. Students who submit ideas to solve environmental problems can win $1,000 grants: $500 to support their ideas and $500 for an environmental internship in their community.

Resources

Books

Green Guide: The Complete Reference for Consuming Wisely edited by Donna Garlough, Wendy Gordon, and Seth Bauer (National Geographic, 2008). A comprehensive resource for green living, with hundreds of pieces of sound information and practical advice.

Keeping a Nature Journal: Discover a Whole New Way of Seeing the World Around You by Clare Walker Leslie and Charles E. Roth (Storey Publishing, 2003). An easy and fun guide to getting people of all ages connected with their own places and landscapes.

Last Child in the Woods: Saving Our Children from Nature-Deficit Disorder by Richard Louv (Algonquin Books, 2008). A thorough investigation of how and why children today are alienated from nature, and what we can do about it.

Organic Crafts: 75 Earth-Friendly Art Activities by Kimberly Monaghan (Chicago Review Press, 2007). Learn how to make creative crafts, games, and activities using natural objects that kids love to collect, from twigs and leaves to pebbles and pinecones.

True Green: 100 Everyday Ways You Can Contribute to a Healthier Planet by Kim McKay and Jenny Bonnin (National Geographic, 2007). A practical guide to the little things we can do every day that can have an impact on the environment.

Web Sites

Agriculture and Agri-Food Canada (AAFC)

www.agr.gc.ca

Provides information, research and technology, and policies and programs to achieve security of the Canadian food system, health of the environment, and innovation for growth. As of May 2009, the AAFC planned to begin certifying organic food produced in Canada. Check the Web site for current information.

Alliance to Save Energy

ase.org

Promotes energy efficiency worldwide to achieve a healthier economy, a cleaner environment, and greater energy security.

American Hiking Society

www.americanhiking.org

Protects and promotes foot trails and the hiking experience.

Arbor Day Foundation

www.arborday.net

Provides numerous resources with the goal of inspiring people to plant, nurture, and celebrate trees.

American Council for an Energy-Efficient Economy

www.aceee.org

Dedicated to advancing energy efficiency as a means of promoting economic prosperity, energy security, and environmental protection.

Bird Sleuth

www.birds.cornell.edu/birdsleuth

Provides detailed information on how students can observe birds, ask and answer their own questions based on observations and data, and share their results.

Break the Bottled Water Habit

www.newdream.org/water

Provides information on the health, environmental, and financial benefits of a bottle-less lifestyle and identifies safe, sustainable alternatives.

Care2's Healthy and Green Living Page

www.care2.com/greenliving

Eco-friendly health and wellness tips, including advice on pets, family life, recipes, gardens, and much more.

Children and Nature Network

www.childrenandnature.org

Created to encourage and support the people and organizations working to reconnect children with nature.

Composting101 Guide

www.composting101.com

A complete home composting guide; offers practical information for converting yard, garden, and kitchen waste into soil-building compost.

Container Gardening

www.containergardeningtips.com

All the information you need to start a container garden.

Defenders of Wildlife
www.defenders.org
A national, nonprofit membership organization dedicated to the protection of all native animals and plants in their natural communities.

Earthwatch Institute
www.earthwatch.org
Engages people worldwide in scientific field research and education to promote the understanding and action necessary for a sustainable environment.

Freecycle
www.freecycle.org
An international network of people who donate and obtain things from each other in an effort to reduce waste, preserve resources, and ease the burden on landfills.

Green Schools
www.greenschools.net
Numerous suggestions on how to take action in your school community in order to make your child's school a greener and healthier place for kids.

Greenpeace

www.greenpeace.org/usa

Works to expose global environmental problems and to promote solutions that are essential for a green and peaceful future.

Greenraising

www.greenraising.com

Information on how to raise "green" funds by providing products that help people consume less, preserve natural resources, and help others.

Kids' Planet

www.kidsplanet.org

A fun, kid-friendly site that gives details on over 50 endangered species, as well as a teacher's table, a "Defend it!" page where children can take action to defend a favorite animal, and more.

Kids Recycle!

www.kidsrecycle.org

Provides tools for kids and teachers to help create zero-waste K–12 schools.

National Audubon Society

www.audubon.org

Learn what you can do to help conserve birds, other wildlife, and their habitats. Click on "Education" to access Audubon Adventures, a page packed with environmental programs and projects to engage children of all ages.

National Wildlife Federation

www.nwf.org

Lots of resources to help regular people confront global warming, protect wildlife, and connect with nature. Also check out www.greenhour.org, NWF's campaign to give kids some time every day for interaction with the natural world. Each week a fresh issue full of activities and information helps guide the exploration and keeps the focus on fun.

Natural Resources Canada

www.nrcan-rncan.gc.ca

Champions innovation and expertise in earth sciences, forestry, energy, and minerals and metals to ensure the responsible and sustainable development of Canada's natural resources.

Natural Resources Defense Council

www.nrdc.org

Works to protect wildlife and wild places and to ensure a healthy environment for all life on Earth. Explore the issues, get the news, and find out how to take action.

No Child Left Inside

www.eeNCLB.org

Dedicated to the passage of the No Child Left Inside Act, this site contains information highlighting the importance of environmental education for our children.

PigeonWatch

www.pigeonwatch.org

A program in which participants observe pigeons and send their data to the Cornell Lab of Ornithology, where scientists compile the information and use it in their research.

Rainforest Alliance

www.rainforest-alliance.org

Works to conserve biodiversity and ensure sustainable livelihoods by transforming land-use practices, business practices, and consumer behavior.

Sierra Club's Building Bridges to the Outdoors

www.sierraclub.org/youth

An exciting program whose goal is to give every child in America an outdoor experience.

Swap-O-Rama-Rama

www.swaporamarama.org

A clothing swap and series of do-it-yourself workshops in which a community explores creative reuse through the recycling of used clothing.

Take a Child Outside Campaign

www.takeachildoutside.org

A program of the North Carolina Museum of Natural Sciences, with partners nationwide, designed to help break down obstacles that keep children from discovering the natural world.

The Daily Green

www.thedailygreen.com

Sign up for the free newsletter and receive daily tips and advice on how to be part of the green revolution.

The Great Backyard Bird Count
www.birdsource.org/gbbc
An annual four-day event that engages bird watchers
of all ages in counting birds to create a real-time snap-
shot of where the birds are across the continent.

The Green Guide to Go
www.thegreenguide.com
A publication of the National Geographic Society, this
is a free monthly newsletter on living the green life.

The Hungry Owl Project
www.hungryowl.org
Learn how to conserve owl habitats and create nest
boxes, and about alternative methods of sustainable
pest management.

Tree People
www.treepeople.org
A resource for improving communities by planting
and caring for trees and educating school children and
adults about the environment. Although based in Los
Angeles, this nonprofit group has valuable resources
for tree lovers everywhere.

U.S. Department of Agriculture (USDA) National Organic Program

www.ams.usda.gov/nop

Details exactly what standards are used by the government for the production, handling, and labeling of organic agricultural products.

U.S. Department of Energy

www.energy.gov

Find energy efficiency and renewable energy information for your home or community with a few quick clicks.

World Wildlife Fund

www.wwf.org

An international organization whose ultimate goal is to create a future where people live in harmony with nature.

Index

About the Author

Judy Molland is an award-winning teacher and writer. She is the author of *Straight Talk About Schools Today* and is contributing education editor for Dominion Parenting Media (formerly United Parenting Publications), the largest syndicate of parenting magazines in the United States. Her articles have appeared in numerous publications, including *Parents, Instructor, New York Newsday,* and the Web site Parenthood.com. She has won a Fellowship from the National Endowment for the Humanities, a Certificate of Appreciation from the California Department of Education, and a Gold Award for Editorial Excellence from Parenting Publications of America.

An avid hiker, backpacker, skier, and rock climber, Judy is a high school Spanish teacher and a leader with her local chapter of the Sierra Club.

Field Notes

More great books from Free Spirit

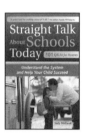